Core Motivation

Copyright 2012 by John Andrew Williams
Academic Life Coaching
Ivy League Coaches, LLC

Portland, Oregon

www.academiclifecoaching.com

Dedicated to Amois,
my love and my bride

February 2012

Contents

Thank You

For introducing me to this work many years ago, I want to thank my mother-in-law, Vicki Hames. She introduced me to this system, otherwise known as the Enneagram, when I was 19.[1] The level of self-knowledge and awareness I developed based Core Motivation has played an essential role in my life.

For their continued support I want to thank my parents, George and Patty Williams. Thanks too for the words ingrained in me as a kid, "You can do whatever you set your mind to." Your belief in me is priceless.

I also want to thank the hundreds of parents and teenagers I have had the honor of working with over the past eight years. Most of this material has come from that work, your sharing your experiences as well as suggestions. Also the thrill of breakthroughs in Life Coaching sessions were a constant source of motivation to continue to bring this work to a wider audience.

---

[1] This book is based on a personality system called the Enneagram. I decided to use a different name than Enneagram for two reasons. First, the pronunciation, ENNY-A-GRAM, sounds confusing and uninviting. When I was using it with High School students it was so much harder to convince them to try an 'Enneagram' than 'Core Motivation' system. Second, the term *Core Motivation* addresses the heart of the system and gives a more accurate description of its use. The system offers valuable information about who we are at our core and what our underlying motivations are.

Thank you too to the dozens of Academic Life Coaches, from Los Angeles to Dubai, who have also used this system and this work with students. I appreciate knowing that it is not just my experience, but that the concepts of Core Motivation cross cultures, personalities, and generational lines seamlessly.

I also want to thank my office staff, Britannie McGurk, Tim Eldredge, and Tara Celantano for their dedication. I want to particularly thank Meghan Sellars for her continued support and outstanding work.

I also want to thank Gina Halsted for her tremendous help in the training programs, proofing parts of this text, and for her feedback and many conversations along the way.

Thank you too to my friends and family who let me run ideas by you. Especially Ben Kaufman, a fellow 7 and avid reader. Thanks for the support and belief in the value of this work.

And finally, I want to thank my wife, Amois, to whom this book is dedicated. I am deeply grateful to you for your love. (Can you believe where we're at!?! And to know that this is only the beginning...)

Thank you,
John

About this Book

This book is designed to help you better understand yourself and others in your life from the point-of-view of Core Motivation. It covers these aspects of Core Motivation:

1) The Definition and Description of the Nine Core Motivation Types

2) Why Core Motivation is so Important

3) How You Can Use Core Motivation in your Life

You will receive some additional tools to help you cultivate a deeper understanding of yourself as well as how to communicate more effectively with others. You will also learn how to become unstuck and quickly recover back to being on top of your game.

I wrote this book for two reasons:

1) Because the concepts in this book have added remarkable value to my life

2) People I had the honor to work with professionally, teenagers and their parents, got the same value from the system

This book began as a series of notes I gave to high school students and their parents to better understand each other and the parent-teen relationship. I do not know of any other kind of relationship with as much potential for friction. If Core Motivation can work for parents and their teenagers, it can work for you.

While passing out those notes to parents and teenagers I was working with, I did not realize or expect parents would also make copies and pass them on to their friends. I would - and still do - receive emails from parents wanting to know their Core Motivation type or more details on how to use the system. Here are the four main queries based on popularity:

1) How can I better understand my teenager?

2) What about my spouse?

3) Are my spouse and I compatible personality-wise?

4) How can I better understand myself?

I wrote this book as an extension of that original seven-page handout to give my best ideas on how I use Core Motivation for myself as well as for my clients. In the process, I hope to try to answer the questions people asked.

I also wrote this book for my friends. I have talked about this book (while writing this book) so much over the last two years that I am thrilled to finally get it out in book form.

Core Motivation & How to Find Your Type

Personality Defined

personality |pərsə'nalitē|
noun (pl. -ties)
1 the combination of characteristics or qualities that
form an individual's distinctive character.
• qualities that make someone interesting or popular.

The word *personality* is derived from the ancient Greek
word *per- sono*. It refers to the mask that actors wore in a
play. Latin picked up the word as *persona*, and it referred to
a *character* and the specific attributes of that individual.

Core Motivation is a personality typing system. It
attempts to accurately describe the primary force of someone
and the usual accompanying thoughts and actions that drive
them. Three points must be clear:

1) We each have unique personalities, characteristics,
and qualities. Typing systems like Core Motivation
merely paint a map or a rough guide to help us be
more aware of our individual characteristics.

2) Our personalities are malleable. Once we are aware
of a certain quality, we can work to change it.

3) As human beings we are much more than a description of our personalities. The nature of being human, however, is well beyond the scope of this book.

For the purpose of this book, I define *personality* as: specific patterns of thought, emotion, and action that make up our character.

What is Core Motivation

Each Motivation Type is a description of those patterns and a realization that we as human beings share a great deal of those patterns. Core Motivation outlines nine general patterns in a system that has roots in ancient wisdom traditions as well as modern psychology.

Everyone has a bit of each Motivation Type in their personality. One of the primary strengths of Core Motivation is its inclusivity: having a strong preference in one type does not diminish that aspect of your personality that may be a different type. You can also have different Core Motivations in different circumstances and as you gain more life experience, you may find that your Core Motivation shifts as well.

However when you read each of the paragraphs describing each type in the section below, one or two types will jump out at you as fitting your personality. Determining your type requires a bit of self-awareness and perhaps the advice and knowledge of someone who has helped type others. If you are still unsure of your type after reading the paragraphs, refer to the section 'Distinctions between Each Type' on page 85.

One last note: we each are individuals, and Core Motivation is just another way to describe to others *what makes you unique*. It is simply one part of a larger description of who you are. No system can capture a unique personality. However, a system can point to different areas to be aware of and consider as you continue to learn more about yourself.

How To Find Your Core Motivation Type

The guidelines for finding your Motivation Type:

- There are nine different styles.

- Everyone has a bit of each style. (A few paragraphs will seem to "fit'.)

- But you are only one core style. (One paragraph will stand out.)

- To find your style, read the following nine paragraphs.

- Choose the top three that describe you.

- Go to page 85 on the section entitled 'How to Distinguish between Two Types.'

- Read each style description and see which one will be most useful for you.

- If you still are not sure, ask friends what they think.

- And if you're still unsure, write me an email: john@academiclifecoaching.com with 'Core Motivation' in the subject line.

Core Motivation Types Described

One: To be Perfect

I like things to be perfect. If I really care about something, I will spend a lot of time working to make it right. I can be extremely organized about things I care about. If only people knew how hard I can be on myself at times! It's as if I have a voice in my head that constantly judges how well I am doing. I don't like errors, and I hate making mistakes. Sometimes I get stressed out at how much I have to do, and I feel like I have to do it right. Others sometime think that I can be serious. I guess I do like to get things done right, but I like to have a good time like everyone else.

Two: To be Giving

I love being able to give to others, and I treasure relationships. At times, I do get worn out and don't pay enough attention to what I really need. At moments like this, I wish I was better at saying 'no' in order to have more time for myself. I love feeling needed and appreciated, especially when someone goes out of their way to thank me. On the other hand, when some people think that I'm trying to control the situation, it hurts my feelings. All I'm trying to do is help!

Three: To be the Best

I want to be the best I can be at what I do. I am very goal driven. I believe that people are what they achieve, and I have achieved a lot. I get frustrated when others waste time or mess it up. Some people call me competitive, and although I admit that I am, I also do well on teams. I tend to care a lot about my reputation and how others see me. When I have a goal I care about, I can focus and get it done. Why do anything if you can't be the best at it?

Four: To be Creative

I love feeling my emotions. Many people consider me creative and artistic. I feel most alive when I express myself and when others understand me. I like to think of myself as unique and different from everyone else. But sometimes I feel misunderstood and lonely. Some say that I am dramatic, but I am only expressing how I feel. I want a deep connection with others. I am after what is true, real, and beautiful. Feelings are extremely important to me. I am what I feel. I don't mind feeling sad. It's a human emotion like any other, and emotions do pass. What's most important to me is that I know what I feel, even if I don't know what to do about it.

Five: To be the Expert

I love being the expert. I like knowing as much as I can about a subject before I have to do anything. I hate it when others say I'm factually wrong when I think I'm right. Often times I would prefer not to answer questions than risk being wrong. I am more than willing to argue my point, and I will reconsider my ideas if the facts don't support what I think. I love going to my room, where I have a space where no one will make demands on my energy or time. I like my alone time. I like to think about past experiences when no one else is around. It helps me sort myself out. I don't like to depend too much on others. In groups, I am more than willing to speak up and say what I want. I enjoy living a simple, straightforward life.

Six: To be Skeptical yet Loyal

I have a good imagination, and I tend to think up worst-case scenarios. That's good because I'm always prepared for the worst. Issues with authority also play a big role in my life. I go from completely going along with those in charge to being a rebel, depending on what I think about them. When someone tells me a new idea, I can usually see what could go wrong with it. I like to think something through before I trust it. Once I trust a person and believe in an idea,

I am a strong ally. People tend to think I'm witty and smart. I have a funny, if unusual, sense of humor.

Seven: To Experience the Best

I want to have the best. I like it when life moves fast and I have a lot of options open. I try to always avoid negative emotion. I run away from being bored, feeling trapped, or being sad. If something does get me down, I'll quickly think of something else. My mind moves 90 miles an hour. I will sometimes get really into a hobby I hardly know about. Then when I get bored with it, I'll drop it. I guess I have a lot of things I've started but don't quite finish. I am good at making connections between things that are completely different. I'm an optimist who believes that life is to be enjoyed. Sometimes I have trouble deciding between two positive choices. Which one will be better? Can I have both?

Eight: To be in Control

I love a good challenge. I love being in control of things that I care about. I am a blunt and honest person who seeks out truth and justice. I respect those in power who treat others fairly. It angers me when people try to manipulate me or act unfairly to others. I like to be in control. Sometimes people accuse me of being bossy, but I'm only trying to make sure everything is ok. I don't like others knowing my flaws or weaknesses. And I have little patience for weakness in others, unless they are trying to make it better. It's a tough world out there. Someone's got to be in control, and I won't hesitate to help those who are not being treated fairly.

Nine: To be Peaceful

I like it best when everything is peaceful. I try to avoid conflict and keep everyone happy. In groups, I tend to go along with what others want. Sometimes I find myself agreeing with someone or something when I don't want to. I sometimes get frustrated with myself, but I don't like to disappoint people. I don't like it when others are angry at each other, and I hate it when people are angry at me. Sometimes people tend to take advantage of my kind nature, but I can stand up for myself when needed. I can usually see all sides to a situation because each side has its pluses and minuses. Sometimes I have trouble knowing what it is I really want. I just want life to be comfortable and peaceful.

Finding Your Motivation Type

Your Top Three Choices that most likely fit you:

1)

2)

3)

If you had to pick just one, which one would it be?

Go to page 85 to find the distinctions between each type.

Why Core Motivation Works

3 Reasons Why Core Motivation Works

Core Motivation works for three primary reasons:

A) **Increases Self-Awareness.** Self-Awareness was a skill prized by the ancients and championed by contemporary psychologists as a necessary component of a high Emotional Intelligence. Core Motivation is a tool to cultivate a healthy awareness of self and use it for personal growth and building strong relationships.

B) **The Same Solution Does NOT Work for Everyone.** People are unique. Being aware of the Core Motivation of a teacher or author, helps you understand their point of view as well as understand that what works for you may not work for them. For example, the advice given to a Type One Perfectionist would vary significantly from that given to a Type Eight Defender.

C) **Motivation, like Life, is a Cycle.** Another strength of the Core Motivation system is understanding that motivation and life have specific cycles. Motivation waxes and wanes. The same personality may look vastly different when vibrant and engaged versus down and bummed out. Core Motivation helps you understand yourself where ever you are in the cycle. Even more valuable, the system will help you recognize the need and provide suggestions on how to quickly recover back to engaged fully with life.

The Big Questions

Self-Awareness boils down to one basic question: "Who am I?" with a tagalong "What am I capable of?"

Life has an amazing way of continually pushing us to understand more about the answers to these two questions.

The quest for answering these two questions goes back to the beginning of abstract thought. For example, inscribed on the Temple of Apollo in Delphi were the words *gnōthi seautón*, translated to *know thyself*. Philosophers from Socrates and Plato to Aristotle and the ancient Greeks understood that knowing yourself was one of the precepts to leading a well-lived life.

Also carved on the temple was *mēdén ágan*, which means *do nothing in excess*. In other words, *don't take yourself too seriously but don't screw up either.*

One way to develop self-awareness is to become more aware of our internal dialogue. Sometimes that chatter is loud. Sometimes, quiet. At times it ceases, and we are totally absorbed in the moment.

We each have our own internal language: the moods, limiting beliefs, empowering beliefs, things that catch us off guard, useless thought habits, and helpful thought habits. We are also (hopefully) aware of things that annoy others. We are certainly (also hopefully) aware of things that annoy ourselves. Knowing your Core Motivation helps you understand your internal conversation and primary driving force.

Learning your personal language is a process that you must do yourself. No one can do the work for you. However, people and books like the one you are reading can help.

The Core Motivation system will help you recognize your vocabulary and patterns in your thoughts, emotions, and behavior. Once you begin to dissect the chatter, you have taken an important step towards being proficient in your internal language. When you can consciously direct that chatter and take meaningful action in your life, you have reached the fluent stage. Such a stage is the rare and precious skill of self-awareness and self-control that the ancient Greeks prized and contemporary psychologists laud.

Unique People, Individual Solutions

The fundamental challenge with transferring information or advice to a large group of people is how to take into account your audience *as individuals*. The nature of attempting such a transfer of knowledge requires that individuals accept the same thinking as the group. Such a demand works well with basic facts like Math, History, and Science, but it does not work well when addressing creativity, interests and passions, or communication.

On a personal basis, advice for one Core Motivation may run completely counter to what is healthy or useful for another type. Knowing yourself and your Core Motivation equips you to understand *your path of personal growth* as well as *common traps for those who share the same type*. You are now aware that following a suggested roadmap that has served someone else well, may actually be detrimental to you. You can also be more alert to seek out those who probably do have the same Core Motivation type and pay more attention to the beliefs they adopted and action they took.

Understanding the Core Motivation Types will prepare you as a reader and listener to better understand by contextualizing the perspective and motivation type of the authors, speakers and teachers with whom you interact. You will understand, without self-judgment, that their suggested method works well for their motivation type, but for you there may be a different answer and solution. The Core Motivation Types do not rest on a hierarchy, but act as tools on an even playing ground in order to locate the individuality we all possess. Understanding your Core Motivation will help you understand yourself and others better and propel you in the right direction.

On a collective level, understanding Core Motivation can help institutions like academia empower students with self-knowledge and increased self-awareness that augments education and prepares students to meet the challenges they will face as adults. The primary challenge facing students in the 21st century is understanding their unique strengths, weaknesses and personality quirks. They also must understand their motivation, leadership and communication styles. *Helping students understand their Core Motivation types reverses the individual to group process. Instead it encourages a process from uniformity to an informed diversity of individuals capable of communicating effectively with one another. I get what you mean here, but these sentences are really funky. Maybe something like Helping students understand their Core Motivation types gives them the individualized self awareness that classroom education can not. It creates a generation of individuals who are capable of communicating effectively with one another.*

I believe this book provides a small but important tool for educators to address increasing Emotional Intelligence and augment the traditional high school curriculum with a priceless skill set.

The Motivation Cycle

The Motivation Cycle is a succession of experiences informed by your Motivation Type. The four points on the cycle are:

1) Engaged - when you're at your most effective and actively engaged in being at your best.

2) Resistance - when something comes up, either internally such as a limiting belief or externally like an unwelcome interruption, stress or anxiety and it pulls you out of being engaged.

3) Disconnected - when you're disconnected and feeling bad about yourself, your situation, or others.

4) Recovery - when you realize you're disconnected, re-engage, and get back in the game.

Engaged

Recovery   Resistance

Disconnected

You can move through the Motivation Cycle in the blink of an eye. Other times it'll take days. The goal isn't to always stay Engaged but rather to recognize each stage in the Cycle and recover quickly if needed. It's impossible to stay at peak performance. Whenever we are up to something - or even when we are not - Resistance will pull us down. It happens, and being Disconnected is a part of life.

Fortunately, if you know your Motivation Type and can recognize the pattern, you can quickly recover back to being Engaged. Here are the three keys: knowing each point on the Cycle, being able to recognize what point you're in, and knowing how you specifically recover.

Engaged

Being Engaged is not just about feeling great and being on top of the world. Even when dealing with something difficult and feeling sluggish, it's still possible. The quality of being Engaged is remaining present to the moment and in the flow of life. It's an experience of understanding that you're literally engaged with reality, being authentic while getting the work accomplished that most needs to be finished.

Sometimes being Engaged is experienced when everything falls into place and you are on top of your game. Life is good. It's not only that something great has happened to you, but you know that you are putting in the effort to make something great happen. Every facet of your personality is working together, and you are leaning into your strengths. Time seems to slow down, and you're absorbed in the moment at hand. Those around you recognize that you are on point, and you are compelling.

Sometimes it's an experience when things become hard. But instead of falling into a default negative pattern, you're able to meet the challenge and address the problem before it spins out of control. Sometimes it's accepting a situation with peace in your heart. At other times it's conserving your energy and taking a well-deserved break. Whatever the situation, you can be Engaged. The trick is to allow yourself to recognize when you're at your best and using all the pieces of your personality by choice, not by default.

The experience feels open, powerful, and peaceful all at once.

As wonderful as it would be to stay Engaged permanently, Resistance will eventually come. It's how we deal with Resistance that really matters.

Resistance

Resistance comes from the Latin word *resistere*, meaning *to stop*. It's second meaning is *to stand up against*. Literally, Resistance *is that which stops us* or *stands up against us*.

In the Motivation Cycle, Resistance is the path which takes us from being Engaged and leads us to being Disconnected. It usually happens quickly - or sometimes we do battle, hanging on to being Engaged for longer and longer periods of time.

Resistance comes from both within and without us. Internally, Resistance shows up as an inner-monologue that usually does one of the following:

- Cajoles us to procrastinate and put a project off into the future.

- Berates us that we are not good enough.

- Scares us.

Internal Resistance can be tough, and it essentially offers us a reason for not doing what we know we need to do. It's unique to the individual but its message is consistent: its goal is to mess things up.

External Resistance is simpler to identify. It could be someone who interrupts your work. It could be a peer, a teacher, a parent, a child, a spouse, an email, a message, a look, or a conversation that jolts you out of being on top of your game.

Both can happen in an instant. Resistance will come. You can expect it. The most useful action to manage resistance is to prepare for it and understand your particular brand of being Disconnected.

Disconnected

Being Disconnected is being stuck in a negative perspective or mood. Sometimes we are able to climb out of it quickly. Sometimes we get bogged down, and it's a slower process. In terms of the Motivation Cycle, being Disconnected is literally losing the link to Core Motivation and to being Engaged.

Losing that connection happens to everyone, and we each have our particular brand of being Disconnected. Whether something external, like a grade, sale, or conversation that didn't go our way, or internal, like just being in a bad mood, being Disconnected is always accompanied by a harsh inner-monologue. Some common examples:

- I'm a bad student/parent/*fill-in-the-blank*.

- I'm worthless.

- I can't do this.

- Other people are cooler than me.

- I'm bad at Math.

- I'm bad at *fill-in-the-blank*.

- This will never work out.

There's a huge difference in making a conscious decision that you're not good at Math and choosing to follow a different academic or career path, and the immediate reaction of being Disconnected that comes from getting a bad grade on a Math test. Being Disconnected feels sluggish. It's frustrating and feels bad.

The trouble is that thoughts while being Disconnected are misleading and false. It's useless to buy into the negative inner-monologue. The negative perspective and typical accompanying mood of being Disconnected heavily influences thought and emotion. Such thoughts and feelings say more about the state of being Disconnected than about reality.

The big problem however, is when action is taken from such a negative perspective. It can lead to a negative self-fulfilling prophecy. The most useful action to take while being Disconnected is to recognize it and to put your energy into Recovering.

Academia, and especially on comments on report cards, emphasizes the concept "full potential." Most young people believe that being in their "full potential" is only when they are feeling great and things are going their way. The truth of reaching one's "full potential" is in the trenches of recognizing they are Disconnected and being able to Recover. It is with this resistance that full potential is realized.

Potential comes from the Latin word *potis* (and ancient Greek word *posis*) which means simply *to be able*. The ability to recognize being Disconnected and Recover back to being Engaged is the single best test of power and ability to reach one's full potential.

Recovery

From the depths of being Disconnected, we each have an opportunity to Recover and get back to the experience of being fully present and Engaged. Recovery is an art form. Generally speaking, it has three distinct steps:

1) Recognize and accept that you are Disconnected.

2) Dismiss the negative self-talk.

3) Do what you know works for you to go back into being Engaged.

Each step in the process can pose a challenge. Pride, the poignant feeling of being justified, and negative habits pose some of the biggest challenges to the first step of being self-aware and humble enough to recognize that we are indeed in the midst of being Disconnected. It takes courage to admit to being Disconnected. Yet it's the first step.

The second step is simply dismissing the negative pattern *as a pattern and not as an accepted view of reality*. It's tempting to look at a situation from the point-of-view of being Disconnected and accept it as being the truth. It's not. Yet arguing with the negative self-talk only further entrenches it. Approaching your thoughts from the point-of-view of a detached observer seems to work best. The most effective action is to simply dismiss these thoughts as if you're physically placing them on the other side of the room and creating as much space between the negative self-talk and yourself.

The third step is to shift your awareness and perspective back to being Engaged with what you know works specifically for you. Planning steps to Recover makes the process smoother, and it's helpful to have a few fail-safes. Some of my favorite are cleaning and organizing, recalling positive sayings, or calling a friend. You will find your own ways, and it's wise to plan ahead.

In the following section, you will find specific recommendations for each Motivation Type, which I hope will serve as a superb starting point to create your own habits for recovering.

Once you've got a foothold on what helps you recover back to being Engaged, the bulk of your work is accomplished. The remaining work is getting in the habit of recognizing the Resistance as well as being Disconnected and Recovering with ease and grace.

Your Core Motivation Type

Core Motivation

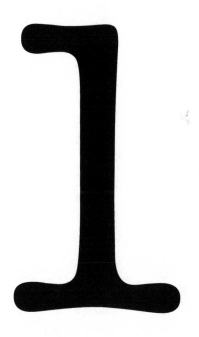

The Perfectionist

One: The Perfectionist

Ones often have a sense of mission and passion about what they want to achieve in the world. They use this passion to create a vision of what's ideal in their own lives as well as the lives of other people. They hold themselves to a high standard. They often hold others to a high standard. They are very much concerned with principle, right and wrong, and sticking to a set of standards at the expense of their comfort.

Engaged

At your best, as a one, you balance your quest for perfection with an understanding that things in your life will never be perfect. You understand that life is a balancing act between what can be perfect and what's possible. You allow yourself to have fun. You go easy on yourself and others. You understand that if you want to do something, you don't need to make it perfect. You just need to make it good.

Resistance

As a one, you find yourself in trouble when you put too much pressure on yourself and others to be perfect.

Here are some examples of Ones meeting resistance:

- Spending way too much time on a project trying to make it perfect even when it's completed and more work isn't really necessary. For instance, tweaking a paper for hours when other classmates probably just spent an hour on it.

- Getting emotional when things aren't falling into place and becoming moody and stressed out.

- Being hyper-critical of yourself and others (especially teachers or partners on a project).

- Thinking that someone wronged you because they couldn't live up to your high standards.

Disconnected

The primary emotion that Ones feel when you are disconnected is anger in the form of being justified or frustrated. You may be angry at yourself for not living up to perfection or the ideal you want. You may be angry at others for not living up to the standards you think they should live up to. Or you may feel fed up with the tremendous pressure of trying to live up to your difficult standards that are nearly impossible to live up to.

Recovery

The key for Ones in recovery is to recognize when you have been too serious and hard on yourself and others. The recovery process for Ones requires recognizing the inner critic and being able to create a separation from the critical voice and to follow your instincts on kindness, understanding and compassion. You're able to maintain a sense of self-discipline balanced with an understanding that you need to take care of yourself and maintain a sense of humor.

Here are some exercises that help Ones:

- When you catch yourself getting angry, think kindness. Recognize your high standards, and also recognize that others do not see the world in the way that you do. Recognize the standards and flexibility in your thoughts that give you your true power and enable you to communicate more effectively with others.

- When you catch yourself trying to make things perfect and getting stressed out, take a moment (and a deep breath), identify how it's perfect right now in the present moment just as it is.

- Identify your inner critic, and learn to put aside the voice that constantly criticizes you and your work. Recognize it as something separate from yourself, and allow yourself to go easy on you and your work.

Core Motivation

The Helper

Two: The Helper
================

Twos find much of their self-worth in how much help they can give to others. They desire to be loved and appreciated, and will go way outside their comfort zone to help others. They often think of others' needs before their own, and can get themselves into trouble when they are overextended and don't take enough care of themselves.

Engaged

When Twos are doing well and feeling healthy they will work for their own fulfillment. Healthy Two's have learned to take care of themselves and to be motivated by a desire to express their own ideas and emotions. They, of course, still care and help others, but it's not to fulfill their own self-worth.

When engaged, Two's balance a sense of the value that they bring other people with what they need for themselves. They can identify their own needs and wants, as well as understand the needs and wants of others, without rushing in and feeling like they have to do something about it immediately. Engaged Twos have a sense of self-worth and don't define themselves necessarily with what they're able to accomplish for others. They've learned to put aside their pride in being able to create so much and understand that they too are human beings and they have their own needs and wants, both of which are valid. They have a sense of satisfaction as well as beauty in their own inner world and their experience.

They're capable of creating a tremendous amount of work and being engaged in their community, while being a bedrock for themselves and other people.

Resistance

Resistance usually comes in the form of feeling resentful. It could be that they have put too much work or energy into helping someone else out and they don't have enough energy for themselves or, perhaps, they don't feel appreciated.

Here are some common forms of resistance for Twos:

- Procrastinating by helping others do their work and then doing their own.

- Only wanting to do well or study a subject because that's what they think will make their parents happy.

- Being so concerned for others that they really don't spend that much time thinking about themselves and what they need.

- Pretending that they don't need any help themselves, but getting really upset if others don't show their appreciation.

Disconnected

When Twos feel that others are not appreciating them and that they've gone outside of their way to help others and have not received much in return they can become blunt and controlling. Twos are especially in trouble when they feel like martyrs. When they feel like they have gone so far outside of their way that they tend to suffer emotionally and physically. Especially if Twos have extended themselves the point of becoming physically ill, it's important for Twos to take a step back and take care of themselves.

To see that their own wants and needs have not been taken care of, they become desperate, even demanding that others attend to their needs.

Recovery

The key for recovering for Twos is to understand that you have to balance your own needs and wants with your desire to help others. It seems the message that much of the culture expresses people should care more about others than themselves gets twisted with Twos. And as a Two you have to recognize that you need to take as much care of yourself as you would other people. Sometimes it's helpful to think of yourself as another person and ask yourself the question, "What would I do to help this person?" Then go ahead and do that thing for yourself.

Here are some exercises that help Twos:

- Draw clear boundaries and learn to take care of yourself. Notice how often you choose to give to someone else even when your energy is low.

- Avoid expectations or thinking that others can live up to your ability to give back. You have a tremendous ability to give. It's sometimes difficult for others to live up to your example. Cut them a break and avoid expectations that others can give back the same way.

- Say what you need, but avoid getting demanding and overbearing. Learn to give energy and love to yourself.

Core Motivation

The Performer

Three: The Performer

At their best, Threes achieve success in many areas of
their life and perform to a high standard. They are able to
take the expectations of other people and mold themselves to
meet those expectations. They find themselves able to walk
into a room or situation and quickly adapt to meet the needs
of that situation. They are highly conscious of what will
look good, and are conscious of what they need to say and
do to fit in. Threes love to get the approval of other people,
as well as the recognition for being the best at what they do.

Engaged

When Threes are doing well, they will feel a certain release from the pressure they put on themselves to always perform to their highest standard, and become a chameleon to garner in the approval of others. They are motivated by the sheer joy of learning more about their personal abilities and stay truer to their own thoughts and emotions while becoming more comfortable, even if that does not match other's expectations.

Resistance

The primary way that Threes meet resistance is by adapting so much to the expectations of other people that they lose sight of what it is they really want for themselves. They often sacrifice their own fulfillment for achievement.

They also may not want to undertake certain projects or get involved in a task if they don't think that they can be the best in the world at it. They can sometimes get themselves in trouble with competition, especially thinking that their actions are going to end up being worthless.

Common forms of Resistance for Threes:

- Only wanting to work on a subject (or a sport) if you know that you can be the best at it.

- Spending impressive amounts of time in one area of your life where you excel at the expense of others.

- Not being clear exactly on what's fulfilling to you, but being acutely aware of what you know other people are expecting from you.

Disconnected

When being disconnected, Threes feel unfulfilled and lost. They may feel exhausted from working hard and frustrated that they are not getting the recognition or approval they desire. They may feel that they are putting all their effort into something they aren't sure is what they want, or someone else wants for them. Struggling with being authentic in their communication, Threes will look to meet the expectations of others and blend into the background, hoping not to be noticed and occupying themselves with busy work.

Recovery

The key for recovery as a Three is to understand that your worth as a human being is not directly related to your performance. Your value goes much deeper than the latest recognition or evaluation of your work. Your value is based on your innate skill set.

In addition, paying attention to what's fulfilling to you and what you intrinsically enjoy is essential. Threes will learn to recover back to being aware of their thoughts and emotions, and, in essence, become loyal to themselves.

Here are some exercises that help Threes:

- Let others know the real you. Trust that they will like you for being you. Allow yourself to disagree with others and to express what it is you're really feeling.

- Notice how often you do something because you think it will look good. Learn to make the distinction between what you want to do because it honors your values, and what you want to do because it meets the expectations of others.

- When working, make sure to take breaks and check in with your energy level. Be aware of pushing yourself hard, which is healthy, and pushing yourself too hard, which is exhausting.

Core Motivation

The Artist

Four: The Artist

Central to Fours is an awareness and attachment to their emotions. Fours have the gift of being keenly aware and attuned to their emotions and comfortable diving deep into emotion - both positive and negative - for longer than any other Core Motivation Type. They use this gift as a source of creativity, their identity as a unique individual and artistic expression. Fours will often feel a deep longing for what's ideal and create unrealistic - although highly romantic - expectations that fuel their emotions. Their self-worth is very much tied up in the affirmation of their emotion, their ability to express what they are feeling and be understood.

Engaged

When Fours are healthy, they can balance their need for feeling their emotions and being in the mood to work to get things done on time. They fully engage in reality by doing work that is meaningful, and get in a habit of staying on top of their work that's assigned. They find pleasure in doing the day-to-day school work, yet still find ways to express their creativity through their work.

Fours have created objective guidelines to provide structure to their work and day and to balance their subjective feelings. They appreciate the present moment - like doing Math homework or finishing a financial report - and give it their full attention.

Resistance

Especially when people don't follow through or make other plans, Fours will often feel abandoned and have a strong emotional reaction. The biggest source of external resistance is when Fours are feeling a strong emotion and others either don't respect, or plain dismiss? their feelings.

Four's internal resistance centers around being hooked to their emotions and taking their subjective feeling about what is or should be as objective truth. In this case, Fours battle feelings of envy and melancholy mostly brought about when experiences do not live up to their expectations. The unmet expectations provide fodder for force to fuel their negative emotion causing Fours to become disconnected from the present moment and those around them.

Disconnected

Fours, when disconnected often withdraw deep into themselves, and use their imagination to fuel the intensity of their motion. They may become dramatic and teary and yearn for others to come to their aid. Once forced to realize that they have withdrawn to themselves and possibly alienated those around them, Fours often shift into trying to be extremely helpful to others. They may go way outside of their way to be thoughtful and generous, hoping to make up for being stuck in their emotions.

Recovery

The central concept for recovery for Four is their ability to balance their subjective emotion with an objective view of reality. Fours must hone their ability to use their innate creativity and desire for expression in ordinary everyday circumstances while doing meaningful work.

Recovery is their opportunity to go back to objective guidelines and temporarily put their emotions on the sidelines.   Here are some exercises that help Fours:

- Beware of feeding your emotions with your imagination and getting caught up in your own world. Recognize that emotions, like the weather, pass. If something is upsetting you, learn to separate yourself emotionally from the issue. Find a pen and paper. Journal. Write a list of pros and cons. Look at real numbers. Then logically determine what's real and get moving into action.

- Create systems that enable you to develop strong habits that support your larger vision. Avoid getting caught up in romantic situations or daydreaming of someone or something coming to save you. Work toward building the life you want step-by-step.

- Set aside time when you give yourself full permission to create and express your artistic sensibility. When you share your art with others, notice how much you expect others to react in a certain way to satisfy your expectations. Expectations are dangerous. Learn to recognize them and set them aside when expressing your art. Your own enjoyment of creating is the reward. The acknowledgement of others is the bonus.

Core Motivation

The Expert

Five: The Expert

Fives love to be right. Much of their self-worth is tied up in being the expert and right in their assumptions about the world. Fives are deeply curious about the world and about subjects that they care about, and may completely ignore or downplay things that they're not interested in. As Fours are very much enthralled with their emotions, Fives are very much attached to their thinking and naturally analytical minds. With often quirky senses of humor, Fives often have a lovable kind of nerdiness that complements their heady way of interacting with the world.

Engaged

When Fives are healthy, they have struck a balance of thinking and analyzing a problem and taking action to create a solution and do the work. They care less about their being right and care more about coming up with, or learning, the right solution. They stop trying to figure out how to do the problem and just jump in.

Resistance

External resistance often shows up when others make demands on a Five's resources or space. Interruptions - especially those that draw on a Five to respond emotionally - can be challenging. Additionally, being proved factually wrong can be devastating. Since Fives tie up their self-worth in their ability to be right, especially the things that they care about, when they get a bad grade or receive a negative report, or are simply wrong about something factual, Fives may stop being engaged and become disconnected and withdraw into thoughtfulness.

Internal resistance often shows up as a feeling of being an outside observer, observing their life going on around them without feeling like they are actively participating. It's as if their mind acts as a buffer between them and reality. Especially if the Five is concerned about being factually correct, they may spend a lot of time thinking about a problem before moving into any meaningful action.

Disconnected

When withdrawing into their mind ceases to work, Fives may become frantic and busy themselves with a multitude of other tasks and projects trying to keep their mind busy and avoid what's really causing them stress. Fives become scattered, disorganized, and increasingly argumentative. They attempt to distance themselves from their feelings as much as possible and isolate themselves from others. Fives may become incredibly stubborn, arguing their opinion and position to absurd lengths in an effort to convince themselves they are right.

Recovery

Fives recover when they allow themselves to make mistakes and not be 100% right about situations and topics, even those they care deeply about and are assumed to be the expert in. When Fives move into action they often bring a certain creativity and thoughtfulness to the problem, and a long-term solution pops up. However, the key for Fives is to take the initial leap into action, and believe in themselves enough to control a situation.

Here are some exercises that help Fives:

- End the ridiculous arguments. Notice how often you tend to identify yourself closely with what you know and how right you are. Also notice when you have the urge in an argument either to sit back and dismiss the other person or engage and argue to increasingly hilarious lengths. Work on your ability to take a deep breath and simply let it go. Let go of the need to be right, and instead focus your attention on what's going to be useful for everyone, including yourself.

- Stop thinking and just do something. Enjoy the time that you spend in your room with all your belongings, but also get out there in the world. Remember to engage with others and remind yourself to be comfortable with taking action even if you don't yet know as much information as you'd like. Relax and let yourself have the experience. Chances are you will enjoy yourself and the experience more than you previously thought.

Core Motivation

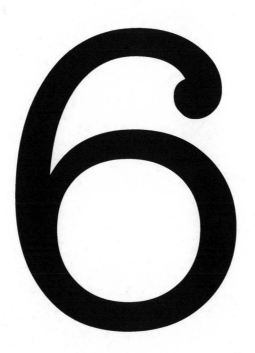

The Friend

Six: The Friend

Central to Sixes is a desire to be safe and counter fear with being extremely prepared for any outcome. To do so, Sixes often imagine the worst-case scenario, and prepare for the worst. Their vivid imaginations are often witty and they have quirky senses of humor. When confronted with a new idea or person, they'll often be skeptical, until they dismiss the negative consequences in their mind. Once they've accepted the idea or person they can be fiercely loyal. It's this quality that makes them outstanding friends. Sixes often don't trust themselves, and build a great support network.

Engaged

When doing really well, Sixes balance being prepared and doing the work with optimism about themselves and the world. When Sixes are healthy they learned to dismiss fears of the worst-case scenario and move forward reliably and consistently to get the job done. They will stay on top of their planner and have habits that allow them to be autonomous and productive, without relying on others to keep them on top of their work.

Resistance

External resistance for a Six is being confronted with a multitude of new ideas or people or situations they need to figure out. Such experiences often bring out a sense of anxiety and a desire to fall back on something they know to be stable. Sixes often search for security and are reluctant to trust someone until they have adequate evidence.

Internal resistance for a Six is often confusion on which direction to take. Often times, Sixes have competing voices in their minds thinking about the best possible situation that would keep them the safest. Fear plays a central role, and Sixes may have a number of limiting beliefs about themselves based on evidence that they haven't been able to follow through completely on what they wanted to.

Disconnected

When a Six feels a deep anxiety about themselves and the environment, they often throw themselves into doing activities and projects to distract them from what's on their mind. Sometimes Sixes can't seem to ever relax, because when they start to slow down and relax, that's when their negative feelings increase. Sixes seem to have an endless stream of projects they can work on, and when stressed out they can be extremely productive.

When stressed, Sixes especially grow more concerned with the expectations of other people and work extremely hard to meet those expectations. At the root of their anxiety is a desire to meet and overcome fear, or being overly cautious and being extremely diligent in their work.

Recovery

The key for recovery for a Six is becoming aware of that voice or their tendency to imagine worst-case scenarios. In its place, Sixes can learn to trust themselves and their instincts. They also learn to nurture relationships with trusted advisors, people who know their natural tendency to think of the worst-case scenario, and can help guide them in their thinking. If the Six can move their worst-case scenario thinking to an optimism about their ability and the ability of those around them to support them, then a Six as well on the path to being engaged with reality in a positive and healthy way.

Here are some exercises that help Sixes:

- When presented with a new idea or meeting a new person, notice your tendency to immediately think of all the negative aspects and worst-case scenarios. Also balance that with thinking about the positive sides and what could be the best possible situation. Most likely, reality will fall somewhere between the two.

- Just for fun, make a list of the worst-case scenarios you recently imagine and feared. File away the list for a couple of months, and put it on the calendar to remind yourself. After two months, open up the list and review what you thought could happen. Usually the list elicits laughter.

- Take a deep breath, and realize your original faith in yourself and your abilities. You can find that you're capable of much more than you imagined, and having a healthy sense of what you're capable of doing, along with an optimism in the future, balanced with your fantastic work ethic will make you fulfilled and successful.

Core Motivation

The Enthusiast

Seven: The Enthusiast

Central to a Seven is an enthusiastic approach to life and its experiences. Sevens tend to be optimistic people, but that optimism masks an underlying fear of boredom and being trapped in unwanted situations. Their minds may move very quickly, mirroring their actions,. and they're able to make connections between things that seemingly have no connection. They battle with thinking that better options are available in making choices and sticking with those choices. Often times, they take on too many projects at once, failing to complete any of them. Sevens want to keep their options open.

Engaged

When Sevens are healthy they will de-emphasize the actual goal and getting what they want and they will put their attention on the work at hand, even finding joy in doing difficult tasks. They will focus on learning more about a subject and sticking with it, even if at times it becomes boring. They learn to work through the boredom and increase their stamina. Sevens realize that putting in the work and creating something productive is the most fulfilling - and fun - they can have.

Resistance

External resistance for Sevens happens when an opportunity arises that might be better than the one they currently have. Sevens often have a hard time making a decision between two positive choices. If they've made a choice that becomes less than optimal, or puts them in a tough situation, Sevens often become disengaged and look for escape. Sevens especially have a hard time when they feel their basic needs, or even wants, won't be met, and feel there's not much they can do about it. And even when they do get what they want, Sevens often battle feelings of being unsatisfied and wanting more.

Internal resistance for Sevens often shows up when they look and see what it is that they want in someone else's life, and compare that ideal to their own circumstances. Sevens tend to exaggerate the positive of the ideal situation and minimize the positive of their current situation. They can often berate themselves for not already being where they want to be. Their minds, seeking excitement, move very quickly on their search for the next great thing.

Disconnected

When disconnected, Sevens feel anxious and strive to avoid pain. They may try to cram their schedules with more tasks than they possibly can accomplish in a day, so that they never feel bored or trapped in any one possibility. When faced with a tough situation, they become increasingly perfectionistic, looking for all the little mistakes and working harder to correct them. Their usual playfulness and creativity melts into gloomy seriousness. They can get increasingly annoyed with their self-imposed limits and distract themselves with those limits rather than completing the work at hand.

<u>Recovery</u>

Recovery for Sevens is threefold. The first is being able to directly address what's causing the anxiety that the Seven is trying to avoid. The second is to recapture that natural playfulness and curiosity about life. The third is to contribute meaningful work to others. Especially when Sevens have a larger mission, that does not have to do with serving their own material needs but helping others, Sevens have a better opportunity to focus their minds and become knowledgeable in one or two areas of study or expertise.

Here are some exercises that help Sevens:

- Pray and meditate. Nothing helps Sevens more than purposeful prayer and meditation to quiet the mind.

- Just say 'No' to your impulses. Notice when you want to stir up the energy in the room and get a reaction from someone just so that you can have a connection. Chill out. Learn to sit back and observe more.

- Embrace boredom. The next time you're bored out of your mind, get curious about how boredom really feels. What does boredom really feel like? Are you more afraid of boredom or the thought of boredom? Be prepared to blow your mind.

- Be here now. Try this experiment for a week: Say 'no' to every thought of a future plan and place your thoughts in the present moment. Sevens tend to get carried away with how fantastic the future will be, and in the process, completely miss out on the richness of the present moment.

- Stop comparing your situation to other's situations. When you think that the grass is greener on the other side, stop. You're exaggerating the positives of the other side and the negatives of your side. To get out of your own way, reverse your thinking. Acknowledge the negatives of the other side and emphasize the positives of your side. You will be amazed at how quickly your anxiety dissolves.

Core Motivation

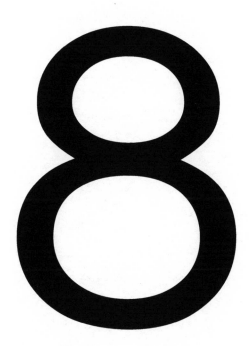

The Defender

Eight: The Defender

At the core, Eights have the desire to be strong and to be in control of one's environment. Eights have a tremendous strength and ability to get a tremendous amount of work accomplished. They love a good challenge. They are natural leaders and feel comfortable taking control of the situation. There's a hard-working edge to them and sometimes people perceive them to be bossy. Eights merely want to make sure they are safe and the situation is under control for themselves and others.

Engaged

When Eights are healthy, they use their immense
strength to be sensitive to the needs of others and are aware
of their impact on those around them. They also allow
others to help them and don't necessarily feel the need to
always be in control. They are motivated by a strong sense
to be at peace with the world and themselves, and they have
balanced their tremendous strength and desire to be in
control with allowing others see their vulnerability. They
lead through example and have a good sense of their
influence on others.

Resistance

Eights thrive on external resistance showing up as a
challenge that needs to be overcome. Especially when
Eights perceived injustice done to others and feel that they
are incapable of helping the situation, they can become
frustrated and angry. Eights also have a challenging time
with authority, especially if they don't trust that authority
figure. Oftentimes, Eights will resist change and help from
others if they feel that in doing so, they have to give up some
control over their life.

Internal resistance shows up for Eights as a deep insecurity about their ability to be strong for themselves and for others. As a result of this fear, Eights will strive even harder to be strong and to express a strong persona. Eights may feel a welling up of power and the desire for revenge that may be challenging for them to manage.

Here are some common forms of Resistance:

- Rushing forward without regard to their own feelings or the feelings of those around them.
- Feeling like others are taking advantage of them or are hopelessly incompetent.
- Putting too much energy into the action, for instance, having a death grip on a pencil while taking a test or typing for hours on a paper without taking a break.
- Taking on too much of the project and not allowing others to see your weaknesses.

Disconnected

For a long period of time, Eights will attempt to push their way through a problem, much like someone using a sledgehammer to break through a brick wall. They can be extremely assertive and argumentative and push hard for what they perceive to be right.

When the challenge is too much, or when they don't believe that they can do anything effective, Eights retreat into their own minds, and stay looking for strategies and ways to even the score. Once they retreat into their minds, Eights who were previously outgoing can become quiet and pensive, even melancholy. It's this point that others around him have learned to fear the most, because Eights have such a means of demanding respect when they're angry over what others around them want.

Recovery

When Eights deeply understand that their power and worth does not come from their ability to get things done with tremendous endurance, but rather in who they are as a human being, complete with their weaknesses and inability, recovery can begin. Once Eights are comfortable sharing their weaknesses with others and understand areas in which they need help, they become incredibly compelling.

The key for recovery for an Eight is to stop blaming themselves and others for their injustices. In essence, to deeply forgive oneself and others in their life. Accept that it's okay to have weaknesses, and it's okay to resign to others for help, just as you use your tremendous power, energy and resources to help others.

Here are some exercises that help Eights:

- As an Eight, you have great power at your disposal: Power of personality, physical power and emotional power. Reflect how you are using that power. Are you using it to help others? Are you using it for your own benefit and ignoring others? Or even worse, are you using your power for revenge? Be honest with yourself and ask the honest feedback of those close to you. As you learn to act consistently for the benefit of others, you will find yourself surrounded by a close group of loyal allies.

- Allow yourself to express your vulnerability and sincerely thank those who help you. Avoid the trap of thinking that you can do everything yourself or that you don't need to rely on others. Expressing your weaknesses does not mean that you're weak, it means that you're human and similar to all of us who are living the best we know how.

- Learn to control your anger and channel the energy into a determination to help others. At their best, Eights are both understanding and compassionate. You must learn the art of forgiveness. Determine what exactly sparks your anger. Write down the negative traits you see in others. Then look in your own life and think of times when you have exactly the same traits. You will surprise yourself. Learn to channel the energy of anger into compassion.

- Learn to dial down your impact to fit the situation. In the past you've had times when you were overbearing, controlling, and didn't take into account the needs of others. Read the room more. Read other people more. By becoming more aware of your surroundings and others, you will find yourself being able to give just the right amount of energy required for the situation.

Core Motivation

The Peacemaker

Nine: The Peacemaker

At the core, Nines have a desire to have an internal as well as external peace. Nines may have such a sense of desire of being peaceful but they don't often assert their needs and wants. They love to stay within their comfort zone. Sometimes they don't know what they really want and rely on the opinions and desires of others. Nines have a natural optimism about themselves and the world around them and they are extremely adaptive and want to do what others expect. Nines also have a hard side to them and can become angry if they feel like they're constantly bending to the wants and desires of others while not taking care of themselves.

Engaged

When Nines are healthy they will have a clear outcome or mission to achieve. They realize the importance of it and are willing to put in the necessary energy. The clarity of their purpose helps them gain the courage to confront others if needed and to step outside their comfort zones when required. They realize that life is more fun, and that they can ultimately expand their comfort zone when they are willing to do what is hard and take reasonable risks.

Resistance

Any demands, especially those that are combative are sources of external resistance for Nines. Nines often have a hard time dealing with argumentative or unpleasant situations and would much rather melt into the background. They sometimes will idealize those around them, and when others fail to meet that idealized version, Nines have a hard time going with the reality of the situation and retreat into their minds, attempting to avoid it.

Internal resistance for Nines shows up as an inability for them to motivate him or herself no matter how hard they try or how bad they desire positive outcomes. For a Nine, they may feel like they're moving through molasses, and they doubt themselves and their ability to accomplish their goals.

They may get distracted, and busy themselves with nonessential tasks.

Disconnected

After going along with the wants and plans of others and withdrawing into their minds, anger often wells up for Nines. Once they're angry, which they go to pains not to express, it bubbles over, and others may be surprised and caught off guard. Nines often get angry at the smallest things, but that anger has been building for weeks.

Thus, when disconnected, Nines often combat their own feelings of being wronged with a desire to continue to be in their comfort zone. The conflict between these two desires gives Nines their ability to scramble to get things done to meet the demands of others, but it often shows up as a certain kind of passive aggressive behavior.

Recovery

The central theme for Nine to recover is to consciously step outside of their comfort zone and be proactive. The central idea for a Nine is that they count. Their ideas, feelings and needs are as real and valid as others. When

Nines feel angry, they can use that as a signal that they need to focus on their comfort zone; more specifically what they need to do to step outside of their comfort zone to be proactive about the situation, before the situation spins out of control. If Nines can learn to use their emotion to spur themselves into proactive action, Nines have an easy job of recovering back to being engaged with their core motivation, and with the reality of life.

Here are some exercises that help Nines:

- Notice what triggers you to seek your comfort zone. What's usually happening around you that prompts you to retreat into your thoughts or want to be in your room. By simply being aware of what's making you want to seek your comfort zone, you're making yourself that much more able to face obstacles, and essentially expand your comfort zone to include taking on challenges and asserting yourself. Powerful ideas for a Nine.

- Keep your mission statement in mind. As a Nine, you have a tendency to put your mission and what's really important to you aside. As you begin to practice action for the sake of your values, what's really important to you, and your mission in the world, you will notice more and more how positive your impact is and how well you are able to assert yourself.

- If you are having trouble in relationships, step back and look at how you have helped create the problem. Nines most often act as enablers, allowing others to take advantage of their peaceful nature. Nines tend be passive-aggressive (not showing up to meetings, not doing homework, taking lots of time to do chores) or blow up when they just can't take it anymore. In your relationship, notice up until now when you used to say 'yes' when you honestly wanted to say 'no.' Notice, too, that when you start saying 'no' when you mean 'no' that you actually help the health of your relationships by being honest with yourself and others. Others will actually appreciate your 'no.'

Distinctions Between Each Type

1-9

<u>One and Two</u>

What they have in common: Ones and Twos both have a desire to help others and be of service. Both can and will go out of their way to help other people.

Essential difference: Their basic motivation for action differs. The primary motivation for Ones is a sense of helping others *because it's the right thing to do*. The primary motivation for Twos, *because they want to build a better relationship*. Ones tend to judge based on their own standards and needs. Twos tend to judge based on other's standards and needs. Ones also tend to feel more independent, while Twos tend to focus on being in a relationship.

Essential Question: Do you desire to help others because it's the right thing to do or because you want to be in closer relationship with them?

It's the right thing to do: One
Want to be in closer relationship: Two

One and Three

What they have in common: Both types can be extremely focused and efficient in getting things done. Both want to achieve high standards of success and improve themselves.

Essential difference: Their basic motivation for action differs. Ones desire to meet their high internal standards of perfection. Threes desire to be the best at what they do. Ones tend to care more about *how* something is done and will stick closely to rules. Threes tend to care more about looking good and being recognized for their achievement.

Essential Question: Do you desire to achieve your own high standards, or do you desire to achieve to be the best at what you do?

To reach own high standards: One
To be the best at what you do: Three

One and Four

What they have in common: Ones and Fours sometimes confuse themselves, because Ones under stress have Four characteristics. Fours, when they are doing well, often display many of the characteristics of Ones. Both types have strengths of idealism and creativity, and a desire for what's real and true. Both types usually wrestle with feelings of guilt, worthlessness, and melancholy; and can become demanding when they feel others do not appreciate them.

Essential difference: Ones usually want to deal with the task at hand, then deal with their feelings. Fours usually want to deal with their feelings, then the task at hand. Ones tend to get upset when others do not follow the rules or fail to live up to certain standards. Fours tend to get upset when others do not appreciate them and do not show enough sensitivity. Ones want to get it right and will push their feelings aside. Fours, on the other hand, will often express their desires and feelings and will withdraw if feeling unappreciated.

One and Five

What they have in common: Both types like to think things through, and both types like to be right about their opinions. Both love knowledge and most likely feel comfortable discussing philosophy. They both will express their thoughts and will defend them vigorously. When thinking things through, both may want time to be alone.

Essential difference: In defending their opinions, Ones tend to get more emotional and irritated. Fives tend to get more detached and will go to extreme, often ridiculous, explanations as to why they are right. Ones tend to think in more practical terms that have a direct impact on improving themselves or their environment. Fives are more concerned with the theory and can become lost in their minds and mental creations. Fives will sometimes create elaborate theories that have no direct relation to reality. Ones tend to judge situations based on their internal standards. Ones think in order to better themselves and the world. Fives think in order to discover more about themselves and the world.

Essential Question: Do you prefer to think in order to reach a more perfect self or to learn more to reach a better understanding of yourself?

To reach a more perfect self: One
To reach a better understanding of self: Five

One and Six

What they have in common: Both types can become anxious and concerned with making sure they are doing things right. Both may often feel guilty when they don't reach their internal standards or when they don't meet the standards others have set.

Essential difference: Ones tend to have strong standards of internal correctness. Sixes tend to rely on outside standards of correctness. Sixes will often not know exactly what they want, while Ones are rarely indecisive.   Sixes try to figure out what could go wrong, while Ones try figure out what's wrong now. Under stress, Sixes often appear more anxious and fearful, while Ones appear tense and self-righteous.

Essential question: Do you often feel more anxious and imagine worst-case scenarios or feel more tense and can point out what's wrong with the current situation?

Worst-case scenarios: Six
Wrong with the current situation: One

One and Seven

What they have in common: Both types have high expectations of themselves, others, and the world. They both like to have things perfect. Sevens under stress will have many of the characteristics of a One. Sevens will get tense and have a high sense of what's not perfect. Ones, when they are doing well, will have some of the characteristics of a Seven: They will feel more carefree and fun loving.

Essential difference: Sevens are usually very optimistic about the future. Ones tend to think of themselves as being realistic and are usually not as optimistic about the future. Ones often display strict self-control and like to have clear rules to follow, while Sevens often get frustrated with rules and limits and will become undisciplined and unfocused.

Essential question: Do you feel like you have a harsh inner-critic or a heightened anxiety to make sure you have the best experience?

Harsh inner-critic: One
Anxiety to have the best experience: Seven

One and Eight

What they have in common: Both types have a strong opinion concerning the way things should be executed. Both types are often concerned with justice and who's wrong and right and what to do about it.

Essential difference: Ones tend to become more attached to the principle of what's right and wrong, while Eights think of themselves more as protectors and will often act to help the underdog in a situation. Eights will directly state their anger and like to be challenged. Ones tend to hint at their anger and push it aside until they can't take it anymore and blow up. Ones tend to persuade others as to why they are right and why this is the best way to do something. Eights tend to simply overpower others with the strength of their personality and intensity of beliefs.

Essential question: Do you believe more on the principle of what's right and wrong or do you more often trust your gut and move to action quickly to protect others?

Rely more on principle: One
Quickly rush in based on gut feeling: Eight

One and Nine

What they have in common: Both types can have a high sense of idealism and can tend to withdraw from others when under stress. Both types will also push their anger aside until they just can't take it anymore and blow up.

Essential difference: Nines tend to push their anger aside for much longer, and will often convince themselves that they really didn't want what they originally wanted. Ones have a much stronger sense of what's right and wrong. Nines tend to like comfort and avoid working hard for extended periods of time. Ones sometimes have difficulty taking breaks and would rather keep working to make it perfect.

Essential question: Do you go to extreme lengths to avoid conflict with others or do you feel a responsibility to express what's right?

Avoid conflict: Nine
Feel a responsibility to express what's right: One

2-9

<u>Two and One</u>
See One and Two.

Two and Three

What they have in common: Both types tend to care deeply about other people and what others think about them. Both types can be extremely outgoing and engage with friends.

Essential difference: Twos tend to focus more on giving to others so that they can be seen as a close friend and someone of value. Threes tend to focus on appearing to be attractive and successful so that others will want to be around them. While Threes appreciate attention, they will sometimes become uncomfortable with others getting to know everything about them. Twos, on the other hand, yearn for close connection and, generally speaking, are more comfortable expressing emotion.

Essential question: Do you tend to focus on relationships and the needs of others or on accomplishing goals and getting recognized?

Focus on relationships and needs of others: Two
Focus on accomplishing goals and recognition: Three

Two and Four

What they have in common: Both types can have intense feelings and focus on relationships. The two types are also connected. When Twos are doing well, they take on more of the positive characteristics of Fours. Healthy Twos will show more creativity and be more aware of how they are feeling rather than having an intense focus on other's feelings. Fours under stress will show some of the characteristics of unhealthy Twos. Stressed out Fours will give and go out of their way for another person in order to earn their love.

Essential difference: Twos are more proactive in reaching out to others in relationships, while Fours tend to emphasize how they are unique and different from others. Twos try to rescue other people and are extremely aware of how others are feeling. Four try to get others to rescue them and are more aware of their own emotional state.

Essential question: Do you feel more comfortable when you are helping others or when you are expressing yourself and others understand you?

Helping others: Two
Expressing yourself and others understand: Four

Two and Five

What they have in common: Both types can care deeply about other people and will often put other people's feelings ahead of their own.

Essential difference: Twos will consistently give more in a desire to be closer in a relationship. Fives can also give much of themselves, but they will also draw back and take time out to protect their personal boundaries. Twos tend to feel more comfortable becoming closer in relationships, but Fives in relationships want to make sure that they still have their alone time.

Essential question: Do you prefer to know what someone is feeling or what someone is thinking?

Feeling: Two
Thinking: Five

Two and Six

What they have in common: Both types can be extremely friendly and go out of their way to please other people. They can be playful and want to be in close relationships with others.

Essential difference: Sixes seek the approval of others in their desire to get their support. Twos seek to be important to others in their desire to be loved. Twos most likely will have a much wider group of people they are close to and share their inner thoughts to, while sixes are much more guarded in who they trust.

Essential question: Do you seek to give to people in order to be loved in return or do you seek to connect with others in order to gain their approval?

Strive to be loved: Two
Strive to gain approval: Six

Two and Seven

What they have in common: Twos and Sevens are often outgoing and can be the life of the party. Both types are comfortable with emotion, enjoy being around people, and have a strong desire to be liked.

Essential difference: Sevens tend to focus on their wants and desires. Twos tend to focus on the wants and desires of others. Twos are much more likely to change themselves to meet the needs of others, while Sevens will attempt to charm others to get what they want. Twos want others to need them. Sevens tend to not want anyone to slow them down or be too dependent on them.

Essential question: Are you more aware of the needs and wants of others, or the needs and wants of yourself?

Of others: Two
Of yourself: Seven

Two and Eight

What they have in common: These two types can easily confuse themselves because they are related. When Eights are doing well they take on the positive characteristics of Twos: They are naturally generous and will use their tremendous energy in the service of others. When Twos are stressed out they show the negative characteristics of Eights: They tend to get demanding and try to manipulate and control the situation. Both types can be extremely warm and friendly and deem relationships as extremely important in their lives.

Essential difference: Anger. When angry, Eights have no problem showing it and letting you know. Twos, in general, have a much harder time letting you know they are angry. While Eights tend to be direct, Twos tend to hint.

Essential question: When stressed, do you most often try to appease the other person or do you most often assert your own wants?

Appease: Two
Assert: Eight

Two and Nine

What they have in common: Twos and Nines both tend to share a positive outlook on life. Both types also have a strong desire to please others, and when pressed, they will most often go along with what others want rather than asserting their own needs.

Essential difference: Nines are happy giving to others and ensuring that others are happy, but they don't necessarily want too much attention in return. Twos, on the other hand, love to be recognized and have others need them. Nines try to avoid others making too many demands on them. Twos thrive on it.

Essential question: Do you find yourself actively going out of your way to help others, or find that you most often help others when it seems easy and comfortable for you to do?

Actively out of your way: Two
Easy and Comfortable: Nine

3-9

Three and One
See One and Three.

Three and Two
See Two and Three.

Three and Four

What they have in common: Threes and Fours are related by the nature of their position. It's possible that someone will be a Three but have a strong Four wing and vice versa. In addition, Threes will tend to blend their identity to whatever they perceive to be most valued. Most often ,Threes will mistake themselves to be fours, especially when they value artistic creativity. It's less likely that Fours will identify themselves as Threes.

Essential difference: Threes have a much easier time putting aside their emotions to accomplish a task. Fours would rather deal with their emotion, then get down to work. Fours often mistake others lack of emotion as shallow, while Threes can get frustrated when emotion slows down getting things done.

Essential question: Would you rather just get the job done, or take the time sort out how you feel then get down to work?

Just get the job done: Three
Sort out how you feel first: Four

Three and Five

What they have in common: Threes and Fives both value accomplishment and more often value thinking over feeling. The most often mistake is for Threes to identify themselves as Fives. This is especially the case when Threes feel pressure, either from teachers or parents to be intelligent. Threes want to live up to that expectation and will mold themselves to fit others expectations. Fives will rarely mistake themselves to be Threes.

Essential difference: Threes tend to care much more deeply about the opinions of others, even if they are reluctant to admit it. Fives, on the other hand, do care what others think of them, but that's much less an important factor. Fives are after knowledge and often need time alone to recharge their batteries. Threes, on the other hand, have an easier time sustaining constant energy, especially when working on a group project or presentation. Threes tend to be more practical. Fives, more theoretical. Threes are much more driven by the bottom-line: what's the point of this process. Fives are much more interested in the process itself and love to think for thinking's sake.

Essential question: Do you tend to be aware of the opinions of others, especially when they concern you, or do you tend to disregard the opinions of others, especially when they concern you?

Regard others opinions of you: Three
Disregard others opinions of you: Five

Three and Six

What they have in common: Threes and Sixes are related, both like to meet the expectations of others, and sometimes have a hard time knowing what exactly they want. When stressed, Sixes will often get hyper concerned about the opinions of others and just want to get moving, not really thinking through what exactly they are doing. When doing well, Threes will show the positive characteristics of Sixes: they will feel comfortable authentically expressing themselves, regardless of how others will perceive them.

Essential difference: Threes tend to be much more comfortable in the spotlight, even thrive in it. Sixes tend to defer attention and get uncomfortable with everyone looking at them. Threes thrive on acknowledgment of their capabilities. Sixes tend to get caught up in worst-case scenarios and take longer to get motivated than threes. Threes get motivated by the recognition they'll receive. Sixes tend to doubt others whey they say they've done a good job on something. Sixes tend to be much sillier than Threes and have a wacky streak that they just can't help expressing. Threes can be silly too, but they more often will conform more closely to social standards.

Essential question: Do you find yourself getting caught up in worst-case scenarios and doubt others when they tell you you've done a great job, or do you often imagine the attention and recognition you will get when you're the best?

Worst-case scenarios and doubt others: Six
Attention, recognition, and being the best: Three

Three and Seven

What they have in common: They both love the best, are outgoing, and highly enjoy success. Both types can be fun to be around and give others a sense of excitement and energy. Both types tend to keep full schedules and stay busy.

Essential difference: The biggest difference is in their core motivation: Threes want to be the best. Sevens want to have the best. Threes are much more conscious of the opinions of others than Sevens. While both care about what others think of them, Threes are much more likely to appear polished and make more socially appropriate statements.

Essential question: Would you rather be the best or have the best?

Be the best: Three
Have the best: Seven

Three and Eight

What they have in common: Both types value accomplishment and are usually eager to take control of a project. Both types can be competitive and will readily say what they think. Both types can appear to be and have everything in control, from their dress, to how they are to the classroom.

Essential difference: Threes are usually much more aware of the opinions of and impact on others, while eights sometimes have difficulty being aware of and turning down the volume on their impact. Eights have a strong desire to be in control and gain more power, changing the world to their will. Threes have a strong desire to be successful and recognized by others for their accomplishment.

Essential question: When trying to accomplish a goal, are you much more likely to change your approach and accommodate to others desires, or are you more likely to express yourself directly and attempt to influence others to your thinking?

Change your approach and accommodate: Three
Express directly and influence others: Eight

Three and Nine

What they have in common: Both types love to please others, love to be liked, and are related. When doing well, Nines will display the positive characteristics of Threes: they will focus and step outside of their comfort zones for the sake of accomplishing a worthwhile project. In contract, then threes are under stress, they often display the characteristics of unhealthy Nines: they become indecisive and lose sight of their own needs and direction in an attempt to please others around them.

Essential difference: Threes have a much stronger focus on accomplishment, and will get frustrated when others get in the way. Nines have a much stronger focus on being comfortable, and will more willingly adopt the goals, needs, and wants of others.

Essential question: When working on a project, are you more likely to keep pushing to be the best at your task, or do you highly value free time and relaxation?

Keep pushing: Three
Value Relaxation: Nine

4-9

Four and One
See One and Four.

Four and Two
See Two and Four.

Four and Three
See Three and Four.

Four and Five

What they have in common: Both can be reflective, intellectual, and appreciative of the details and beauty of an object. Both types tend to be introverts and like spending time alone in which they can get caught up in their internal worlds. Both can be highly individualistic and spurn conforming to the standards of society. True loners of Core Motivation, Fours and Fives can feel completely content when alone and occupied with their own thoughts and emotions.

Essential differences: Fours get caught up in the world of their emotions. Fives get caught up in the world of their thoughts. Fours tend to be much more emotive, while Fives tend to recognize that they have emotion but want to think about their experience than feel the emotion.

Essential question: Do you most often find yourself caught up with an emotion or a theory?

Emotion: Four
Theory: Five

Four and Six

What they have in common: Both types tend to consider themselves as highly individualistic. And both types rely on their emotions and can be extremely aware of feeling unsure of themselves. Both types have a tendency to get caught up in negative emotion at times and can have a hard time moving past doubt and fear.

Essential differences: The core motivation differs: Sixes are alert to what could go wrong and want to avoid it. Fours are aware of what's missing and want to have their longing fulfilled. Fours focus on their own emotional state before the emotional state of others. Sixes tend to focus on what others are feeling before they tend to their feelings. Fours are usually more individualistic and want more alone time than sixes.

Essential question: Are you more aware of what could go wrong in the future or more aware of what's missing now?

What could go wrong in the future: Six
What's missing now: Four

Four and Seven

What they have in common: Both types tend to rely on their emotions and get caught up in maintaining certain emotional states. Both types can be intense and highly romantic - idealizing experiences that they would like to have. Sevens and Fours are often quick to know what they want or what could make the situation better.

Essential differences: Sevens try to avoid negative emotion at all costs, and although they feel sad at times like everyone else, they will quickly look for ways to distract themselves and feel better. Fours simply accept negative emotion as a part of life and have a tendency to indulge in melancholy.

Essential question: Do you tend to accept feeling sad as simply a part of life or try to avoid it at all costs?

Accept as part of life: Four
Avoid at all costs: Seven

Four and Eight

What they have in common: Both types can have intense feelings, and can attempt to persuade others on the force of their passion.

Essential differences: Eights and fours have an extremely different approach to feelings. When faced with negative emotion, Eights will get tougher and just keep moving forward. Fours, on the other hand, have a difficult time letting negative emotion go, and tend to want to dwell in emotion and make sense of it before moving forward. Eights often feel vulnerable, but unlike Fours, they try to avoid showing their vulnerability.

Essential question: Would you rather just get the job done or figure out how you are feeling first?

Get the job done: Eight
Figure out how you are feeling: Four

Four and Nine

What they have in common: Both types tend to be
introverted and treasure their alone time. Both fours and
nines also have a tendency to lose focus and need time to
recollect their energy before moving forward.

Essential differences: Fours withdraw to nurture their
emotions and often want to intensify what they are feeling.
Nines withdraw to protect their energy and time, and would
prefer to rest in their comfort zone. Nines also have a much
easier time blending their wants to those of others, while
fours usually feel comfortable being much more
independent.

Essential question: Would you rather express your true
feelings or blend your feelings with others.

Express true feelings: Four
Blend feelings with others: Nine

5-9

Five and One
See One and Five.

Five and Two
See Two and Five.

Five and Three
See Three and Five.

Five and Four
See Four and Five.

Five and Six

What they have in common: Fives and Sixes are both intellectual and love to think things through before they make their decision. Gathering more information and learning more appeal to both types.

Essential difference: Sixes tend to think more practically; Fives, more theoretically. Fives also are more non-linear in their thinking. Sixes tend to analyze to find the problems and ponder what if scenarios. Fives will think to create new ideas and concepts as to how it all fits together or why something works. When faced with a challenge, Fives tend to withdraw and become cooler in their reaction, while Sixes usually become more intense.

Essential question: When faced with a challenge do you usually become more intense and think of "what if" scenarios or do you like to take a step back and calmly think through all the possible solutions?

More intense and what if scenarios: Six
Take a step back and think through possibilities: Five

Five and Seven

What they have in common: Both types love learning and finding out more about a subject. They both can be highly energetic and have an eccentric side of their personality.

Essential difference: Fives seek knowledge and understanding. Sevens seek excitement and new experiences. Fives like much more alone time and like taking a step back to think about a situation. Sevens like to plunge right in, and although they appreciate some alone time, they like to be in the middle of the action. Sevens are more optimistic than Fives. Fives are more realistic than Sevens.

Essential question: When faced with a challenge do you instantly try to see the positive side to the situation or do you like to take a step back and think it through?

See the positive side: Seven
Take a step back and think it through: Five

Five and Eight

What they have in common: Both types are concerned with their energy and resources. They are wary of authority, although they value respect and fairness. When stressed, Eights will often withdraw and take on many of the characteristics of Fives and strategize their next step. When feeling secure, Fives will feel comfortable enough to step out and take a big risk in moving a project forward.

Essential difference: Fives plan. Eights act. Fives usually take a much longer time moving into action than Eights. Eights will often act, then think. Fives like to think things through first. Eights can be extremely practical and don't want to be bothered with why something works. Fives usually love knowing the reasons why something works, and if it actually does or does not is sometimes an afterthought.

Essential question: Do you like to move into action quickly, thinking on the run, or would you prefer to think out all your steps out in detail first?

Act quickly: Eight
Plan out steps: Five

Five and Nine

What they have in common: Both fives and nines are the true introverts of Number Typing. Both value time alone in which they can preserve their energy and time. They often get uncomfortable with many of the demands of others. More often nines will mistake themselves for fives than vice versa.

Essential difference: By their nature, nines have a more difficult time identifying themselves as any one type, and often nines are attracted to the description of spending time alone and wanting to preserve their time and energy. The main internal motivation for Nines is to remain peaceful and comfortable. The main internal motivation for Fives is to understand and have as much knowledge as possible. Fives tend to like detail, while Nines are more comfortable with the bigger picture. Nines usually trust people readily. Fives are naturally skeptical. Nines tend to create happy scenarios in which everything works out in the end. Fives tend to create elaborate scenarios with both pros and cons to any likely outcome.

Essential question: Do you prefer to think in broad terms and go along with the opinions of others or would you rather spend time thinking about the details and reaching your own conclusions.

Broad terms and going along with other's opinions: Nine

Details and reaching own conclusions: Five

6-9

Six and One
See one and six.

Six and Two
See two and six.

Six and Three
See three and six.

Six and Four
See four and six.

Six and Five
See five and six.

Six and Seven

What they have in common: Both types can be extremely witty, funny, and a little eccentric. Both can come across to others as anxious and thinking about things too much.

Essential difference: Sixes tend to see the worst-case scenario while sevens tend to see the best-case scenario. Sixes think of what could go wrong so that they can be prepared. Sevens think of what could go right and distract themselves from what could go wrong but underneath is still an underlying anxiety. Sixes tend to stick with projects and career choices much longer than sevens.

Essential question: When thinking about a challenge, do you think of what could go wrong and how you can be prepared, or do you imagine what could go right and how much more you'd enjoy it?

What could go wrong and how you can be prepared: Six
What could go right and how much more you'd enjoy it: Seven

Six and Eight

What they have in common: Both sixes and eights often react to anger by dealing with it directly. Both types rely on their instincts, can be fiercely loyal, and tend to root for the underdog. Both have an inherent distrust of the world and like things to be proven throughly before believing in them.

Essential difference: Sixes react more out of fear. Eights react more out of instinct. When challenged, eights will push ahead and keep pushing while sixes tend to become more fearful and eventually self-defeating. Sixes tend to be more passive-aggressive. Eights, simply aggressive. Sixes will try to avoid conflict and seek to blend in while eights can be calculating in their response and will direct seek to escalate conflict if it suits them.

Essential question: When faced with a challenge do you usually welcome it and push harder, or do you experience moments of doubt but move forward anyway?

Welcome it and push harder: Eight
Moment of fear but move forward anyway: Six

Six and Nine

What they have in common: Both types like to be safe and comfortable. Both will seek the opinions of others when making decisions, especially big decisions. Both like to live up to the expectations of others.

Essential difference: Sixes have a difficult time not showing when they are upset. Nines can remain cool and quiet, but eventually, when they can't take it anymore, react in anger. Sixes tend to be immediately suspicious of others. Nines tend to be immediately trusting of others. When stressed, nines will take on the characteristics of a six and doubt and mistrust people and think of the worst that could happen. When doing well, sixes will take on the positive characteristics of a nine: they will feel peaceful and trusting of the world and those around them.

Essential question: Do you trust people easily, almost to a fault, and have an easy time remaining calm when upset, or do you naturally doubt people at first but then become extremely loyal and have an easy time expressing yourself when upset?

Trust people to a fault: Nine
Naturally doubt at first but then become loyal: Six

7-9

Seven and One
See one and seven.

Seven and Two
See two and seven.

Seven and Three
See three and seven.

Seven and Four
See four and seven.

Seven and Five
See five and seven.

Seven and Six
See six and seven.

Seven and Eight

What they have in common: Both types can have a lot of energy and lose awareness of their impact on others. Both will directly go after what they want, and like to get what they're after.

Essential difference: Eights enjoy being in control and will happily take on responsibilities even if it limits their options but means they'll have more control. Sevens also enjoy being in control, but the primary motivation is to have the best experience. If that means someone else is running the ship and they get to sit back and have fun, sevens will happily choose that option. Eights accept pain as a part of life and move forward anyway. Sevens try to avoid pain at all costs or reframe the pain in a positive light.

Essential question: When confronted with pain do you most often try to view avoid it and plan for how it's going to be alright in the future, or do you get down to business and deal with it directly?

Plan for how it's going to be alright in the future: Seven
Get down to business and deal with it: Eight

Seven and Nine

What they have in common: Both are optimists, like life to be happy and comfortable, and remain pleasant even in the face of difficulties. Both types attempt to ignore the negative side to situations, although Sevens are much more intense about doing so.

Essential difference: Sevens tend to be extraverted, love excitement, and when trying to recharge, Sevens often will attempt to become busier. Nines tend to be introverted, like it when things are calm and peaceful, and when trying to recharge, like to be alone and quiet. Nines try to maintain a feeling of peace. Sevens try to maintain a feeling of excitement.

Essential question: Do you try consistently to feel peaceful or excited?

Peaceful: Nine
Excited: Seven

8-9

Eight and One
See One and Eight.

Eight and Two
See Two and Eight.

Eight and Three
See Three and Eight.

Eight and Four
See Four and Eight.

Eight and Five
See Five and Eight.

Eight and Six
See Six and Eight.

Eight and Seven
See Seven and Eight.

Eight and Nine

What they have in common: Both enjoy life to be comfortable and take great joy in the simple pleasures of life.

Essential difference: Eights thrive on conflict. Nines hate conflict. Eights willingly take on challenges and move quickly into action. Nines like to make sure that the challenges they take on won't force them too far outside their comfort zone.

Essential question: When faced with conflict, do you directly address it, or do you try to avoid it?

Directly address it: Eight
Try to avoid it: Nine

9

Nine and One
See One and Nine.

Nine and Two
See Two and Nine.

Nine and Three
See Three and Nine.

Nine and Four
See Four and Nine.

Nine and Five
See Five and Nine.

Nine and Six
See Six and Nine.

Nine and Seven
See Seven and Nine.

Nine and Eight
See Eight and Nine.

Made in the USA
San Bernardino, CA
30 August 2016